This book of poetry mostly dives deeply into emotions felt after a breakup with someone who felt so incredibly like the future. A vast look into what real and unconditional love is like, something new and magical and unfortunate to lose.

ABOUT THE AUTHOR

Amanda grew up a quiet gal who spent many hours reading and writing. Typically poetry has not been something she has dipped her toes into until the last few years. Amanda is mostly a generic journal writing type, and if anything, expected to write a book of short stories because of her wild dreams!

Amanda has a degree in Environmental studies, and Psychology. So creative writing is a huge leap in familiar topics for her.

Wonderings

James Grosser

Wonderings

James Grosser

Presentation by *BookLeaf Publishing*

Web: www.bookleafpub.com

E-mail: info@bookleafpub.com

ISBN: 9789357615549

First edition 2022

Dappled Light

I sit beside my empty page,
Dimly lit by a flickering light.
My words fail to flow
So i sit; at peace.

Perhaps this is a trap,
A cunning one no doubt.
For it hides itself in shade
And frees not he who seeks

To find himself in lyric,
For that is the delay.
Perhaps I need more light,
Or less for it is day.

So I will take my leave of it.
I will greet my bed.
Its true it may be warm
Yet fails to free my head.

Around and around,
Spinning in the dappled light.
I haven't moved for an hour.
Is everything alright?

Faded

The scars that once seared my skin
And bled and stung
The tears that burned my cheeks
And choked out my words.

They are now but little marks,
Their former power now unrecognisable.
Why then do the new pains
Sting with their same ferocity?

Perhaps it is like an autoimmune response
The old, long forgotten scars burning,
Trying to stave off
New ones from forming.

A 'visit from the teacher' of sorts
A reminder from my mind
To close the door
And stay hidden.

Caring Apathetically

You need my help again?
I'm sorry I can't -

Okay, I'm coming.

No it's okay I promise.

No it's nothing really.

You've called me 6 times.

But I'm okay.
If you think the weight
You press on with such force
Will have me crack—

You're probably right.

But I don't care.

No, I do care
Perhaps that is the problem
I don't feel like caring
But I do regardless.

I will be there.

Hummingbird

Fleeting bird, for a moment
I captured your attention.
As you had for so long held mine.

I remember for months,
You would catch my eye.
Giving meaning to menial tasks,
As I would watch you through my kitchen
window.

And in some foolish way,
I left my window ever so slightly
Ajar.

At first I was greeted
By moths, wasps and the occasional bee.
Despite these unwanted guests
I kept it open.

Hoping perhaps you would notice me
As I had so often noticed you.

Then one day, despite having lost hope;
Moments away from closing my window
You flew in.

You stayed,
We danced, we sang
And as the day grew long
Your soft feathers nestled into my hands.

When I awoke,
You were gone.

I ran to the window,
And there you were.
I waved with panicked enthusiasm
And off you flew.

Goodbye my Hummingbird.

Mushrooms

When I was very young,
I loved mushrooms.
In particular the delicious
Ones made with garlic butter.

Once, just once
I had with them
An experience
So horrific

That now even their smell
I am unable to tolerate

And so they have become a tool
Of my self loathing and my hate
I eat them when I drink,
And when I feel I can't escape

But the feeling of disgust
So deep, a pit of my mistakes.
I punish myself with mushrooms
I hope you do not do the same.

The Pursuit of Truth

I don't tell lies
But is omission the same crime?
My father told me
The worst sin
Is lying to oneself

So what is the truth?
I ask myself;
My emotions surely
Deny it.

The pursuit of truth,
One of our greatest struggles.
The Truth, My Truth, Our Truth
What do any of these mean?

Am I a pessimist?
A solipsist?
A narcissist?
I hope not.

If I believe it to be true
Is that enough
Is telling a non-truth
Equally damaging with intention than without?

Equally damning?
Is an attempt at honesty enough?
I hope so.

Tongues

We speak in tongues,
The words we say
Have no meaning;
Not the meaning intended.

You say sweet nothings
But your eyes say it all;
You needn't scream, or dance,
Or cry.

Truth, or lie
We each speak to something,
Something deeper in each other;
Aura's intertwined.

You know when I am broken,
You know when I am sick.
When I am tired or hoping
For something I can't admit.

So hold your secrets,
Hold them close.
I'll hold mine.
In truth,
there's nothing we can hide.

Edward

I hate Edward,
He torments me,
All of my darkest moments
Have been his doing.

He screams at me
Shouting with such force
I can't hear even my own thoughts.

He crushes me,
His weight preventing any breath
From reaching my lungs.

He reminds me when I am alone,
And somehow convinces me,
I am even more so when surrounded by friends.

There are few who can stave him off.
I gave up long ago.

Sometimes he will leave for a while.
Even the devil needs a holiday I suppose.
I experience the strangest calm in his absence.

It's although a part of me is missing;
Though I hate to call him that.
I've grown so accustomed to his noise,
His weight.

In his presence I am broken,
In his absence I am lost.

Blame

Humanity's greatest fantasy
Isn't Gods, Angels or Spirits;
Some higher power
With each of our interests at heart

Nor is it the foolish hope
That prevails
Despite any number of horrors and fears

No, our most foolish creation,
Is an evil greater than ourselves.
That temptation, blame, and any of
other of our many shortcomings

Can be attributed to some demon,
Devil or dark entity.

The statement that is most true
Is also the one most sobering.
There is no one to blame for this,
But ourselves.

Selective Presentation

I see you
smiling, laughing, crying
I see you
hiding, shouting, lying

I see you,
but it's all a game,
you see me,
and its all the same

I see you,
when everything is fine,
I see through
only half the lies

I see you,
when I hold you crying
I see you,
even when your lying

They tell us,
comb your hair
straighten your tie
else someone see behind your eyes

We all choose what we want them to see
sometimes i wish
we'd all just be.

Chasing

Chasing something
that is pretend;
a memory,
a forgotten friend.

Your quaint light
never fails
to catch the eye,
the colours bright

Deep in I breathe
and deeper still
the flavour of your warm air
is comforting.

And as i watch
you slowly fade
from green to yellow
yellow to red.

I'll miss you till
you take your rest.
May you live on
like all the rest.

I Hate Food

Is my pain real, tangible,
If it manifests not, on my skin?
If the cuts and burns lie only on my brain?
If tears can no longer roll down my dying grey
cheeks?

I can smile anytime, anywhere.
Tell me you need me, it's like a switch.
I feel the snake wrap around my chest
he drags me back into loneliness

I hate food.
It reminds me of my body,
that is not mine, I lost it.

My struggle?
I want to be alone,
Not lonely.

Broken

People seem to love me
Cause I'm good at fixing broken things.
Things they thought were hopeless,
And hopelessly obsessed with fixing.

I figure out my worth,
the love I deserve
by the things I fix.

But what they fail to see
Right up until it's too late,
Is even if I don't mean it
I'm just as good at breaking things.

Enjoy your heart once I've pieced it together,
Because its glass.
It won't last a minute,
Don't give me the chance.

The hammers always waiting
And the pieces fall apart.

Night Visions

What is the creature
I watch through glass
With silv'ry hue

He shows not love
A cold repute
Perhaps he is lost

It has been too long
Since he has cried
Since he has smiled
Since he had died.

I feel a deepened sadness
As the lights turn out
As does he

He failed to see
The light in which he stood
And now it is gone;
he is cold

I wish I could save
His glazed eyes
From what they have already seen

It's too late for that now
as he lies
Wondering what might have been

Take Note!

Take Note!
I hate you,
Should I give out a reason?
Doesn't sound like something you'd do.

But I am not you.
So don't forget
This kind courtesy
I offer your foul head.

Your nose is too long,
Your heart too small
You trip over duck feet
and blame anyone at all

Well, maybe you'll grow up.
Maybe you won't
I'd wish you the best
But insincerity.
I don't

In Between

Im dripping again,
Well every time
I fill the cracks
More falls through
Is this an act?

Do I stand up
Or stay down here
I've always known
The lines weren't clear

When your role
Is to fill, like mine
You're always in between

I can't stand
To close my eyes
Else I miss
What I could have seen.

I'm Sorry

It's the little things you know
The ones that throw my heart too and fro
It's less the things you do,
Rather it's the things you don't

I suppose I am rather fragile
My trust so fractured
Even the slightest nudge sends it back
To the pieces in which it now belongs

Entropy is natural I suppose
I know I'm lying in chaos
Am I draining you again?
I'm sorry

I will stop.
Soon.

Words in My Ears

You do find it
So terribly exciting
To twist your words
Into lies

And yet it's just to me
Your code allows nothing else
Only my ears
May be burned by your words

The fire spreads
Down through my head
Through my blood
Infests my heart

The shaking never stops
Not truly.
I can't trust your words
Until you let go

Let go of the false narrative
That these lies protect me
These lies infect me
Don't you see

I wish it was different
I wish I could say
You've always been honest
True to me

But ever since we were little
You chose pre-tense
You chose to lie
To burn me inside

I hope it stops
One day soon
Please try to stop
Else something soon

Will come of it
You can't control
And I can't either
Let me go.

Pessimistic Observance

Are we capable of change?
Every day I'm more afraid
that is not a human trait.
because every time I hear it,
I see people stay the same.

Do you dare to lie again
right to my face, does it end?
I can't tell what time it is
I lost count after all these years.

Each of you is all the same,
you may have a different suit
a different name.
But your interests never stray
Protect what there, destroy the change.

Droplets

Like a child
I watch the droplets race
I took great pleasure in such absent thought
when I was younger
so why not now?
A half-smile crosses my lips as another droplet
forms,
does this new life have a chance against those
already half-way down the window?

I always was excited
when a droplet 'took out' another.
Perhaps I am more of an optimist than I thought.
it is those who bring other raindrops with them
that always win.

We drive on, the rain stops suddenly
as if it were time for a new lesson;
a new reflection.
I close my eyes for a second and am reminded of
why I keep them open.
Staring until my eyes bleed is the lesser of two
evils

As the car slows and halts

I feel a moment of sadness,
regret.
Have I wasted this journey?
Let it be not so again.
This journey is mine alone.

So like the raindrops on my window
I will run,
picking up who I can.
May we help each other
win the race.

I Hate

I hate avoiding your eyes
Sitting so close,
Yet so so far away.

I hate ignoring your smile,
Your laugh,
Your cry.

I hate pretending
That everything's great,
Everything fine.

I hate that I can't feel anything
Not now,
Not tomorrow.

I hate that I can't change
What I said
Or how I said it.

I hate this feeling of loneliness,
An empty void,
I can't escape.

I hate being divisive

Intolerant.
Scared.

I hate being this shell
Of who I was
Let alone who I could be.

I hate living this lie.

I wish I could come back.

I can't even cry.

www.ingramcontent.com/pod-product-compliance
Lightning Source LLC
LaVergne TN
LVHW021354200726

843509LV00014B/2855